100
DESERT WILDFLOWERS

Janice Emily Bowers

WESTERN NATIONAL PARKS ASSOCIATION
TUCSON, ARIZONA

ACKNOWLEDGMENTS

100 Desert Wildflowers is based on numerous articles in scientific journals; too many, unfortunately, to cite each one individually. Without the work of these many scientists, however, I could not have written this book. I also thank Steven P. McLaughlin, Stephen L. Buchmann, and Betty Fink, who read the manuscript and contributed ideas and comments.

Published by Western National Parks Association. The net proceeds from WNPA publications support educational and research programs in the national parks. Receive a free Western National Parks Association catalog, featuring hundreds of publications. Email: info@wnpa.org or visit www.wnpa.org

ISBN-10 0-911408-72-X
ISBN-13 978-0-911408-72-0

Written by Janice Bowers
Edited by Abby Mogollón
Designed by Nancy Campana, Campana Design
Cover Photograph George H.H. Huey
Printed by Imago
Printed in Malaysia

Warning: Many of the plants in this book can be found on public lands such as national parks or nature preserves, where plants and animals are protected by federal law. Please do not pick wildflowers. Leave them for others to enjoy.

THE SETTING

What is a desert? A simple answer is that deserts are regions of scanty and irregular rainfall. In the arid southwestern corner of North America, an area that includes parts of California, Utah, Arizona, New Mexico, Texas, and adjacent Mexican states, rainfall varies from a few inches to as much as nine or ten each year.

Some years more than the average might fall; other years rainfall might be almost nonexistent. In the deserts of southeastern California, most rain falls during the winter, in western Texas most in the summer. In Arizona, midway between these two extremes, rainy seasons occur in winter and summer. As with annual totals of rainfall, much variation in the timing of rainy periods can and does happen.

Ocotillo blooms

Clint Farlinger

But a desert is more than a place where rain falls rarely and irregularly. What else makes a desert? Scarcity of plants, for one thing. In many parts of the desert, rocks rather than plants dominate the landscape. Scanty and unpredictable rainfall means that permanent water is rare in the desert, and most streambeds are dry except after heavy rains. Desert summers are notoriously hot. Air temperatures fluctuate greatly during the course of a day and night, particularly during the winter when freezing nights often give way to balmy days.

Sonoran Desert wildflowers

Bruce Griffin

Owl's clover and marigolds

Randy Prentice

Biologists and geographers recognize four major deserts in North America: the Sonoran Desert of southeastern California, Arizona, Sonora, and Baja California; the Mojave Desert of southern California, southern Nevada, and northwestern Arizona; the Chihuahuan Desert of southern New Mexico, west Texas, Chihuahua, and Coahuila; and the Great Basin Desert of Utah, Nevada, eastern California, southeastern Washington, and southern Idaho. This book concentrates on wildflowers in the deserts of Arizona and adjacent states.

For ease of reference, the wildflowers depicted in this book have been arranged by color. To learn about related species, look for plants that have the same family name.

THE DESERT IN BLOOM

Desert wildflowers invariably mean spring wildflowers, for the plants that bloom in the summer are less numerous than those of spring and, on the whole, not as colorful. It's hard to predict exactly when the desert will bloom—or if it will. In Arizona, spring arrives first in the low desert along the Colorado River and spreads gradually eastward. Altogether, the vernal season lasts about four months, from February in the Yuma area to April and May around Tucson.

When the desert blooms abundantly, it is a sight never to be forgotten. In some places, you can wade in wildflowers to your shins, even to your knees. You can lie supine in a field of wildflowers and disappear from view as bees buzz over your nose on their untiring search for nectar and pollen. In such springs, when the usual drab greens, grays, and tans of the desert

Mexican poppies and lupines

Randy Prentice

are blanketed by a patchwork of magenta, blue, orange, white and yellow, it's hard to remember how the desert looks most of the time.

Why does the desert bloom so sporadically? Most spring wildflowers in the desert are annuals—they live out their brief lives in a matter of months, then die. They must be sown from seed anew each year like garden annuals. Seeds of desert annuals are quite particular in their requirements. If the soil is too dry because not enough rain has fallen, they won't germinate. If the soil is moist, but the winter has been too cold or too warm, they won't germinate either or will germinate only in low numbers. During some years the combination of moisture and temperature is just right for certain wildflowers but not for others. In other years a small area will burst into gorgeous bloom while the surrounding countryside is relatively barren. But in the finest years, when the temperature and rainfall requirements of many species have (at long last) been fulfilled, entire counties seem a mass of bloom, and the air is filled with the buzzing of bees and the clicking of cameras. It's said that such an ideal year comes once every three or four decades.

Strict germination requirements are a kind of insurance for the seed, keeping it from germinating when it isn't likely to survive to maturity. Spring wildflowers have also adapted to the desert by growing only during the time of year when most of us love to be in the desert. Like tourists who leave the desert as soon as the weather turns hot, wildflowers too give up once spring is past. Their brief lives are an accommodation to the harsh demands of year-round life in the desert.

FLOWER VISITORS

While looking at desert wildflowers, you'll probably enjoy watching the animals that visit them. As far as most plants are concerned, the main purpose of flowers is to attract insects and other visitors that pollinate the flowers by transferring pollen from the anthers of one flower to the stigma of another. Most plants prefer cross-pollination; that is, movement of pollen between plants. In fact, many will not set seed if the pollen is transferred between flowers on the same plant. Such self-pollination is usually not to the long-term advantage of a plant. In the desert, however, many wildflowers can pollinate themselves and often do when pollinators are scarce.

Most of the flower visitors you'll notice will be bees of one sort or another. You'll no doubt recognize the familiar honeybee; the stout, black carpenter bee; and the black and yellow bumblebee, but many others might be unfamiliar. Almost all desert bees are solitary, living singly instead of in colonies as do honeybees. Solitary bees make their nests in tunnels in logs or soil. They lay a few eggs in special cells inside each tunnel, providing pollen for the larvae to eat once the eggs hatch. Moths are also important pollinators, particularly the large sphinx moths sometimes called hawkmoth. These heavy-bodied moths hover as they feed from flowers after dark. Unlike bees, which visit flowers for pollen, nectar, and, rarely, oil, moths come only for nectar. Other flower visitors you might see include a variety of butterflies, beetles, wasps, ants, flies, hummingbirds, and bats. Not every visitor is useful to the flower: some simply rob pollen or nectar without pollinating the flower in return. Many flowers have evolved structures that minimize such theft.

A WORD ABOUT PLANT NAMES

Though common names can be delightfully descriptive and informative, they are entirely unstandardized. Most plants lack widely accepted common names. A few, however, have several, and to add to the confusion, some quite different plants even share the same common name. Fortunately, every plant has only one valid scientific name that is shared by no other plant. Though scientific

Anna's hummingbird
and a fairy duster flower

C. Allan Morgan

names are an essential tool for botanists, they can be a stumbling block for wildflower enthusiasts. This need not be. Many people are afraid to pronounce the cumbersome Latin or Greek names, not realizing that they already know and use dozens of scientific names already. Geranium, chrysanthemum, phlox, poinsettia, zinnia: all are scientific names. Moreover, not all botanists pronounce Latin or Greek names alike, and if *they* aren't in perfect accord, why should anyone else worry about it?

Scientific names have three parts. The first part, the genus name, corresponds roughly to your family name. The second part, the species name, corresponds to your first name. Just as your first name distinguishes you from the other members of your immediate family, so the species name of a plant distinguishes it from every other species in the genus. The third part of every plant name is the authority—the surname of the botanist who first described the plant as a new species. If a later botanist decides the plant belongs to a different genus, as sometimes occurs, his or her name becomes part of the authority, too. Often these surnames are abbreviated. Few botanists bother to memorize the authorities of every plant they know, and you don't need to worry about it either except to realize that the authority is part of the complete scientific name. The scientific names used in this book incorporate the most recent changes in nomenclature, according to the U.S. Department of Agriculture. You may know some of the plants in this book by older names.

CONSERVATION

It's important to know that many plants in the Southwest are protected by law and may not be cut or dug up. All cacti, yuccas, and agaves are protected, as are ocotillo and all the wildflowers that grow from bulbs. In parks and monuments, every plant is protected. Remember, no plant will thrive in your hands the way it will thrive in its native soil.

Bruce Griffin

1 · Desert Onion

You'll recognize the desert onion immediately by its odor: crush one of the long, narrow leaves between your fingers and inhale the chivelike fragrance. The pale, pink-striped, six-petaled flowers appear in the spring on rocky slopes. Wild onions, like their cultivated relative, grow from bulbs, though the domesticated onion is much fatter and juicier than the wild ones. Desert onion bulbs grow eight to twelve inches below the soil surface, often wedged among rocks where they are hard to root out.

Steven P. McLaughlin

SCIENTIFIC NAME	*Allium macropetalum* Rydb.
FAMILY	Lily
RANGE	From western Colorado and eastern Utah to southern Arizona, New Mexico, and Texas

2 · Desert Lily

Randy Prentice

The long, undulating leaves of the desert lily (also called the ajo lily) appear on pebbly or sandy flats as early as February in a good spring. Within a month or so, the plants send up foot-high stems bearing large, white, trumpet-shaped flowers that resemble Easter lilies. Hawkmoths, attracted by the intensely sweet fragrance, are probably the most important pollinators of the flowers. Native peoples of the Southwest ate the bulbs, which grow deep beneath the soil surface.

SCIENTIFIC NAME	*Hesperocallis undulata* Gray
FAMILY	Lily
RANGE	Southwestern Arizona, southeastern California, and northwestern Sonora

3 · Palmilla

Almost the only part of the palmilla that the southwestern Indians did not use was the dry, woody seed pods. The vitamin-C-rich flowers provided food; the leaves supplied fiber for baskets, sandals and nets; and the roots when soaked in water produced shampoo. The cleansing properties of palmilla led to its alternate common name of soaptree. The large, bell-shaped, white flowers appear in May and June.

SCIENTIFIC NAME	*Yucca elata* (Engelm.) Engelm.
FAMILY	Agave
RANGE	On plains in desert and desert grassland from southwest Texas to southern Arizona

Randy Prentice

4 · Joshua Tree

Joshua tree flowers, which appear between March and May, have an amazing sex life. Female moths of the genus *Tegeticula* gather balls of pollen from the anthers, then lay their eggs inside the small, green ovary of a yucca flower on another plant. After a moth has deposited her eggs, she rubs the ball of pollen into the stigma of the flower. As the ovules mature into seeds, the moth eggs hatch into small caterpillars that eat the developing seeds. Both the moth and the Joshua tree are winners by this arrangement. The flowers are ensured pollination, and the moth is certain that her offspring will have a steady food supply. The Joshua tree loses a few seeds to the developing caterpillars, but this is a small price to pay since enough seeds survive to perpetuate the species.

Bruce Griffin

SCIENTIFIC NAME	*Yucca brevifolia* Engelm.
FAMILY	Agave
RANGE	From southern California to Arizona and Nevada

5 · Flat-top Buckwheat

Flat-top buckwheat, a shrub about two feet tall, is equally at home in desert or chaparral, and is often abundant on burned-over slopes. The narrow, leathery leaves minimize water loss, an important consideration in the dry habitats where the plants grow. When flat-top buckwheat blooms between March and June, its small white or pink flowers are visited by bees, which make excellent honey from the nectar. Flat-top buckwheat is one of about 120 species of wild buckwheat *(Eriogonum)* in the greater Southwest. The genus *Eriogonum* is, in fact, one of the largest in our area, and new species are still being discovered.

Janice Bowers

SCIENTIFIC NAME	*Eriogonum fasciculatum* Benth.
FAMILY	Buckwheat
RANGE	From southern California to Arizona and Nevada

6 · Anemone

Anemone is an ancient Greek name from a word meaning wind. In fact, anemone is sometimes called wind-flower. Most anemones grow in alpine and subalpine habitats, but ours is a desert wildflower common on rocky slopes, especially on limestone and basalt. Technically speaking, anemone lacks petals. Instead, the sepals, which are green and inconspicuous in most flowers, are white to pink and quite showy. Anemone blooms early in the spring.

Janice Bowers

SCIENTIFIC NAME	*Anemone tuberosa* Rydb.
FAMILY	Crowfoot
RANGE	From Texas to Utah, Arizona, and California

7 · Cream Cups

The delicate flowers of cream cups, a spring-flowering poppy, produce no nectar, but small solitary bees come to them anyway for the copious pollen. Cream cups is so variable that as many as sixty different species have been proposed. Although most, if not all, of the cream cups in Arizona have entirely white petals, some in California have white petals with yellow centers or yellow tips or even completely yellow petals. Contemporary botanists find it most convenient to regard all these variations as different forms of the same species.

SCIENTIFIC NAME	*Platystemon californicus* Benth.
FAMILY	Poppy
RANGE	From Arizona to southern Oregon

8 · Prickly Poppy

The large, white, wrinkled petals, the single eye composed of yellow-orange stamens and the bristly stems and leaves make prickly poppy instantly recognizable. The petals are nearly the only part of the plant that lacks prickles: even the flower buds bear sharp thorns. In all likelihood, however, it isn't the prickles that deter cattle from eating prickly poppy so much as the poisonous yellow sap. Because cattle avoid prickly poppy, the plants increase rapidly on overgrazed ranges, and dense stands of prickly poppy

are one indication that the land has been abused. Prickly poppy grows along roadsides and in pastures throughout the West. It blooms nearly year-round.

SCIENTIFIC NAME	*Argemone pleiacantha* Greene
FAMILY	Poppy
RANGE	Throughout the West

SCIENTIFIC NAME	*Dithyrea californica* Harvey
FAMILY	Crucifer
RANGE	Southern Nevada, western Arizona, and California

Named for the bilobed fruit that looks like a pair of eyeglasses, spectacle pod is a common annual wild-flower on dunes and sandy flats. The seeds germi-nate following winter rains, and the sweetly scented flowers appear in the spring. Spectacle pod is found in southern Nevada, western Arizona, and California; a closely related species (*Dithyrea wislizenli* Engelm.) grows from Utah to Chihuahua.

Steven P. McLaughlin

Around Tucson the urn-shaped blossoms of twist flower are always cream-colored. Farther west in the Ajo Mountains of Organ Pipe Cactus National Monument, a form with lemon-yellow flowers is more common, and to the east in west Texas and New Mexico, most twist flower plants have lavender blos-soms. Botanists have discovered that flower color isn't always a useful guide in distinguishing one species from another. A better criterion is whether or not plants from different populations are interfertile; that is, can we successfully pollinate the stigmas of a cream-colored twist flower with pollen from the anthers of a lavender one? Greenhouse experiments have shown that this is indeed quite possible, and botanists have concluded that all three belong to the same variable species. Twist flower is a spring-blooming annual.

C. Allan Morgan

SCIENTIFIC NAME	*Streptanthus carinatus* C. Wright ex Gray
FAMILY	Crucifer
RANGE	Southern Arizona, New Mexico, and western Texas

11 · Catclaw

Sometimes it seems that everything in the desert bites or pokes or stabs or stings. Catclaw contributes materially to this impression. Its numerous thorns are shaped like a cat's claw and readily catch onto flesh, hair, or clothing at the slightest touch. The brushy, cream-colored flowers of catclaw are delightfully fragrant, and desert beekeepers consider them to be an excellent nectar source for honey. A small tree or large shrub, catclaw can be found most often in desert washes. Catclaw blooms prolifically in May; in some years, scattered flowers also appear in August. Catclaw is more frost tolerant than many acacias.

Janice Bowers

SCIENTIFIC NAME	*Acacia greggii* Gray
FAMILY	Pea
RANGE	As far north as southern Nevada

12 · Sand Blazing Star

C. Allan Morgan

Sand blazing star, one of the prettiest of the blazing stars, is a spring-flowering annual of sandy washes and pebbly slopes. The cream-colored petals are streaked inside with pale orange lines; these are nectar guides for insect visitors, mainly bees. Following the nectar guides to the center of the flower, a bee pushes apart the many stamens and descends headfirst into the floral tube. In the process, the bee's head and underside become dusted with pollen. Though the bee scrapes much of this pollen into her pollen basket, some remains to pollinate flowers on neighboring plants. The leaves of this and other blazing stars stick to almost everything they contact and feel like sandpaper to the touch. This rough, adhesive quality comes from numerous tiny, barbed hairs.

SCIENTIFIC NAME	*Mentzelia involucrata* S. Wats.
FAMILY	Loasa
RANGE	Southeastern California to southern Nevada, western Arizona, and Baja California

13 · Ghost Flower

The creamy blossoms of ghost flower, their centers spotted with brick red, superficially resemble those of sand blazing star, which are creamy and streaked with pale orange. Both ghost flower and sand blazing star bloom in the spring and often grow side by side in sandy washes or on gravelly hillsides. The resemblance of ghost flower to sand blazing star is so close that even bees are sometimes fooled. Whereas sand blazing star provides nectar and pollen for bee visitors, ghost flower offers nothing. But by the time a bee has worked its way into the floral tube of a ghost flower and has discovered that the blossom contains no nectar and little pollen, the bee has already inadvertently pollinated the flower.

Larry Ulrich

SCIENTIFIC NAME	*Mohavea confertiflora* (A. DC.) Heller
FAMILY	Loasa
RANGE	Southeastern California to southern Nevada, western Arizona and Baja California

14 · Saguaro

The famed saguaro, or giant cactus, is one of about fifty genera of columnar cacti found in deserts and thorn forests from Argentina to Arizona. The saguaro's great height, up to fifty feet, and tremendous weight, up to nine tons, is supported by a skeleton of about two dozen spongy, wooden rods. Accordion pleats enable the plants to expand and contract as they gain and lose moisture. Each white flower opens after nightfall throughout the month of May and closes by late afternoon the following day. The abundant nectar attracts solitary bees, honeybees, nectar-feeding bats, and white-winged doves. Bees are probably the most important pollinators now that bat populations have been decimated by pesticides. The fleshy red fruits, avidly eaten by a variety of birds and mammals (including humans), are sometimes mistaken for flowers from a distance.

Randy Prentice

SCIENTIFIC NAME	*Carnegiea gigantea* (Engelm.) Britt. & Rose
FAMILY	Cactus
RANGE	Arizona, Sonora, and near the Arizona border in southeastern California

15 · Christmas Cactus

The pallid flowers of the Christmas cactus attract less attention than the bright red berries. Appearing in May and June, the flowers give way by August to the ripe, pulpy fruits. In December, the fruits still cling to the branches, giving the plant its common name of Christmas cactus. The narrow, spiny stems of adjacent plants sometimes twist together in tangled, impenetrable thickets. Diamond cholla, which resembles Christmas cactus but has stems incised in a diamond pattern, is found from southwestern Utah and Nevada to Sonora and California.

Bruce Griffin

SCIENTIFIC NAME	*Cylindropuntia leptocaulis* (DC.) F.M. Knuth
FAMILY	Cactus
RANGE	From Texas to Arizona and Mexico

16 · Teddy Bear Cholla

This is one teddy bear you won't want to hug. It may hug you, though; the joints detach readily and latch onto any careless passerby. (Should you find that a cholla joint has latched onto you or your dog, use a comb to detach it.) This detachability works to the advantage of the cholla, for loose joints often become rooted and grow into new plants. In this way, teddy bear cholla forms thickets on sandy flats or rocky slopes. Though people and dogs must treat teddy bear cholla with respect, certain desert packrats—also called wood rats—handle the prickly cylinders with impunity. Because the fur and footpads of these packrats resist penetration by cholla spines, the animals can use the joints to build their dens. Packrats also depend on cactus pulp for food and water; they discard the spines before they eat the moist flesh.

C. Allan Morgan

SCIENTIFIC NAME	*Cylindropuntia bigelovii* (Engelm.) F.M. Knuth
FAMILY	Cactus
RANGE	Southeastern California to southern Arizona and northern Mexico

17 · Dune Evening Primrose

Randy Prentice

SCIENTIFIC NAME	*Oenothera arizonica* (Munz) W.L. Wagner
FAMILY	Evening Primrose
RANGE	Sandy places from Oregon to Nevada, Arizona and northwestern Mexico

Opening around sunset and wilting by mid-morning of the following day, the fragrant blossoms of dune evening primrose attract a variety of hawkmoths. The long tongues of these stout-bodied moths are well suited for probing the one-and-one-half-inch-long floral tubes for nectar. (The floral tube is the long neck that connects the petals to the ovary.) As the moth hovers before an open flower, it brushes against the stamens, and long threads of pollen stick to its legs and underside. When the moth moves to the next flower, the pollen threads catch onto the very sticky stigma. Little in nature goes to waste, and certain species of solitary bees collect the leftover pollen early the next day before the flowers wilt. Because the pollen grains hang together in sticky threads, they are difficult to handle, and bees that depend exclusively on evening primrose pollen possess specially modified pollen bristles for collecting the threads.

18 · Brown-eyed Evening Primrose

SCIENTIFIC NAME	*Camissonia claviformis* (Torr. & Frém.) Raven
FAMILY	Evening Primrose
RANGE	Utah, Nevada, southern California, Arizona, and northwestern Mexico

Janice Bowers

In southern Arizona, the flowers of this evening primrose are white with dark centers. Farther west other varieties have yellow flowers. The blossoms open late in the after-noon, and soon afterwards small, solitary bees visit the flowers for pollen and nectar. One species of solitary bee, *Andrena rozeni*, the primary pollinator of brown-eyed evening primrose, collects pollen from no other plant. These bees also mate among the blossoms of brown-eyed evening primrose, and the sandy places where the plants grow provide suitable nesting sites for the bees. Hawkmoths do visit brown-eyed evening primrose if dune evening primrose is not available, but their long tongues enable them to extract nectar without pollinating many flowers. Brown-eyed evening primrose, an annual wildflower, blooms in sandy places in the spring.

_19_ · Desert Milkweed

Even at seventy-five miles an hour, you can't help but notice desert milkweed when it blooms along highways in the late spring. The individual flowers, borne in large, spherical heads, are composed of an inner circle of tiny upright sacks, called hoods, and an outer circle of flat, triangular petals. Milkweed pollen comes in teardrop-shaped packets known as pollinia. You can sometimes remove a pair of the pollinia by carefully inserting a needle between two hoods. These pollinia are highly specialized so that they clip onto the legs of insect visitors, then unclip when the insect visits another milkweed flower. Sometimes small insects become trapped by the clips and cannot leave the flower. The tarantula hawk, a large blue and orange wasp often seen taking nectar at desert milkweed in the spring, is strong enough to be an effective pollinator. Desert milkweed grows along roadsides and in washes.

SCIENTIFIC NAME	_Asclepias erosa_ Torr.
FAMILY	Milkweed
RANGE	Southern Utah to southeastern California, western Arizona, and northwestern Mexico

_20_ · Climbing Milkweed

This milkweed is a vine that clambers over trees or fences. You'll find it in desert washes or as a weed in city lots. The pink or white flowers smell like onions and attract a variety of butterflies and bees. The long, white hairs that cap each milkweed seed enable the seeds to float through the air with the slightest breeze. During the Second World War, milkweed fluff was used as a substitute for kapok in life preservers; because the hairs are hollow, they make excellent insulators and are remarkably buoyant.

SCIENTIFIC NAME	_Funastrum cynanchoides_ (Dcne.) Schlechter ssp. _cynanchoides_
FAMILY	Milkweed
RANGE	Western Texas to southern Arizona and northern Mexico

21 · Leafless Milkweed

Like many desert perennials, the leafless milkweed bears leaves only after rains. During the rest of the year, the green stems manufacture the sugars needed for growth. Like many other milkweeds, the plants contain a milky sap rich in cardiac glycosides, a class of compounds that acts upon the heart. Too large a dose of glycosides can be fatal to livestock and humans. Surprisingly, caterpillars of the monarch and queen butterflies thrive on milkweed foliage. The poisons they eat make them poisonous to predators—mainly birds. As adult butterflies, monarchs and queens retain the toxins ingested as caterpillars, and birds learn to avoid them. Leafless milkweed grows along roadsides and in ditches. It blooms in the spring and again in the summer if rains have been adequate.

Steven P. McLaughlin

SCIENTIFIC NAME	*Asclepias subulata* Decne.
FAMILY	Milkweed
RANGE	Southern Nevada to northern Mexico

22 · Narrowleaved Popcorn Flower

Of the several dozen species of popcorn flower in the Southwest, the narrow-leaved is one of the most common. The tiny white flowers and coiled stems are typical of most popcorn flowers, so botanists identify the different species mainly on the basis of seed characters. Most popcorn flowers can pollinate themselves, which is a good thing since few pollinators can work the narrow blossoms. Small solitary bees in the genus *Proteriades* use special, curling bristles on their mouth parts to extract the pollen without enter-ing the flower. No doubt these bees do effect some pollination as they move from plant to plant. Narrowleaved popcorn flower blooms in the spring in sandy places.

Steven P. McLaughlin

SCIENTIFIC NAME	*Cryptantha angustifolia* (Torr.) Greene
FAMILY	Borage
RANGE	Western Texas to southern Nevada, Arizona, southeastern California, and northern Mexico

23 · Desert Broom

Quick to appear after soil disturbance, desert broom thrives along highways, on abandoned dirt roads, on burned-over slopes, and in washes. Like many desert perennials, desert broom survives without leaves much of the year. The inconspicuous white flowers appear in the fall. Since the male and female flowers of desert broom grow on separate plants, flowers are fertilized as wind blows pollen from the males to the females. Although flowers of desert broom aren't particularly noticeable, the dandelion-like fruits are impossible to miss in the late autumn as they sail through the air like snowflakes and accumulate in drifts against obstructions.

C. Allan Morgan

SCIENTIFIC NAME	*Baccharis sarothroides* Gray
FAMILY	Sunflower
RANGE	Southwestern New Mexico to southern California and northern Mexico

24 · Desert Star

SCIENTIFIC NAME	*Monoptilon bellioides* (Gray) Hall
FAMILY	Sunflower
RANGE	Southern Utah, Arizona, southern California, and Sonora

Clint Farlinger

Desert star flowers always have yellow centers, but the rays vary from white to pink to lavender. Some desert wildflowers, including desert star, are called "belly flowers" because you have to get down on your belly to appreciate them. At its best, a single plant sports up to a dozen flowers on ground-hugging stems. At its worst, a single flower *is* the entire plant. This plasticity of growth is an important survival technique for desert wildflowers when rains have been sufficient for germination but not for luxuriant growth. The ability to bring just a flower or two to seed under adverse conditions is typical of many desert wildflowers. Desert star grows on pebbly flats.

25 · Spreading Fleabane

This annual daisy feels at home from the desert to the pine forest. It is common on dry slopes, along roadsides, and in vacant lots throughout western North America. The hairiness, leaf shape, and size of spreading fleabane vary greatly from plant to plant and place to place, which is not surprising, given its wide distribution. Indeed, spreading fleabane is so variable that one botanist, Edward L. Greene, described various forms at least three different times under three different names. Greene, an Episcopal minister who eventually left the ministry to devote all his time to botany, held no truck with Darwin's evolutionary theories, published in *The Origin of Species* in 1859. Greene firmly believed that species had remained unchanged for eons. This rigid view made him unable to recognize the variability in spreading fleabane and led him to describe even slight variants as new species. Most modern-day botanists find it convenient to take a broader view.

Janice Bowers

SCIENTIFIC NAME	*Erigeron divergens* Torr. & Gray
FAMILY	Sunflower
RANGE	Throughout western North America

26 · Desert Zinnia

Rick and Nora Bowers

At first glance, desert zinnia doesn't look much like a member of the sunflower family. The white rays number only four to five, making each flower head look more like a poppy than a sunflower. Still, each ray is a separate flower, as are each of the six to eight tubular flowers in the center of the head. Desert zinnia can be abundant on plains with creosote bush and white thorn. It also colonizes abandoned dirt roads and thrives on soils rich in calcium carbonate (lime). Desert zinnia blooms after rains in the spring and summer.

SCIENTIFIC NAME	*Zinnia acerosa* (DC.) Gray
FAMILY	Sunflower
RANGE	Texas to southern Arizona and northern Arizona

27 · Plains Blackfoot

Rick and Nora Bowers

SCIENTIFIC NAME	*Melampodium leucanthum* Torr. & Gray
FAMILY	Sunflower
RANGE	Kansas to Arizona, Texas, and northern Mexico

You might confuse desert zinnia with plains blackfoot since both have white rays and yellow centers. They're easily told apart, however: a desert zinnia flower head has only four or five ray flowers, whereas plains blackfoot has about twice as many. In the Southwest, plains blackfoot grows most abundantly on limestone. It blooms in spring and again in summer.

28 · Fremont Pincushion

An abundant wildflower following good winter rains, Fremont pincushion features heads composed entirely of white or pinkish disk flowers. Within each head, the flowers vary in size: those on the outside are markedly larger than the ones in the center. Fremont pincushion commemorates John C. Frémont, explorer, self-promoter, and territorial governor of Arizona. Although primarily a politician rather than a botanist, Frémont collected plants during his travels, and he is remembered in the genus *Fremontia*, among other plants. He discovered Fremont pincushion on his 1843 journey from the Missouri frontier to the Columbia River and back again, during which he mapped two routes to the Pacific Coast and crossed the formidable Sierra Nevada several times. Although his collection of Fremont pincushion was little more than a fragment, it was enough to enable the great Harvard botanist Asa Gray to recognize that the plant was unknown to science, and Gray named the little annual in honor of its discoverer.

Steven P. McLaughlin

SCIENTIFIC NAME	*Chaenactis fremontii* Gray
FAMILY	Sunflower
RANGE	Throughout southern California and southern Nevada to southern Arizona

29 · Tackstem

Tackstem is easily told from the desert dandelion, which it closely resembles, by the tack-shaped glands on the stem just below the flower head. This desert annual is named *Calycoseris wrightii* after Charles Wright, who discovered it growing on rocky hills near El Paso in the spring of 1852. At the time, Wright was one of the topographical engineers assigned to the United States and Mexico boundary survey. A graduate of Yale, Wright had earlier knocked about, teaching and surveying as the opportunity arose and collecting plants wherever he went. The large collection he made while working on the boundary survey was an important addition to botanical knowledge. Tackstem blooms in the spring.

Steven P. McLaughlin

SCIENTIFIC NAME	*Calycoseris wrightii* Gray
FAMILY	Sunflower
RANGE	Western Texas to Utah, Arizona, southern California, and northern Mexico

30 · Desert Dandelion

Janice Bowers

Especially abundant on sandy flats, desert dandelion is a common spring wildflower from southern California and Arizona to Idaho. Like many desert ephemerals, desert dandelion doesn't appear every spring but waits for the right combination of rainfall and temperature. If you look closely at a flower head, you'll notice that all the flowers are alike. Unlike the common sunflower, which has both ray and disk flowers, desert dandelion has only ray flowers. The genus name of desert dandelion, *Malacothrix*, comes from the Greek words for soft hairs and refers to the fluff on the mature seeds.

SCIENTIFIC NAME	*Malacothrix glabrata* (Gray ex D.C. Eat.) Gray
FAMILY	Sunflower
RANGE	Southern California and Arizona to Idaho

𝟹𝟷 · Desert Agave

Steven P. McLaughlin

SCIENTIFIC NAME	*Agave deserti* Engelm.
FAMILY	Agave
RANGE	Southeastern California and southwestern Arizona to Baja California and northern Sonora

The desert agave, sometimes called a century plant, doesn't live nearly as long as a century. When the plants are eight to twenty years old, they send up a single, sturdy flowering stalk, then after the flowers have set fruit, the entire plant dies. Desert agave leaves, like those of all agaves, grow in rosettes. Although the leaves are armed with stiff terminal spines and sharp marginal teeth, this didn't deter desert-dwelling Indians from digging up the rosettes, trimming off the leaves with stone tools, and roasting the remaining chunks in rock-lined pits. Baked agave, a nutritious energy source rich in sugars, can still be purchased in Mexican markets. Desert agave is one of the most drought-tolerant of the 136 species of agave found in North America. It grows on rocky slopes and gravelly plains. The plants bloom in June, and the dried flower stalks with their panicles of hard seed capsules remain conspicuous for many months afterward.

𝟹𝟸 · Golden Smoke

Not strictly a desert plant, golden smoke grows from Pennsylvania to Alaska and south to northern Mexico. In the Southwest, it thrives best in disturbed spots such as washes, logged-over woodlands, old burns, and pastureland. The tiny white cap on each seed is a food body that contains a milky fluid rich in lipids—that is, fats and oils. For certain kinds of ants, food bodies are far preferable to the seed itself. Ants that collect seeds of golden smoke keep the food bodies and discard the seeds, thus dispersing golden smoke from place to place. This is an example of mutualism: the ants gain a source of food and the plants gain a means of dispersal.

Janice Bowers

SCIENTIFIC NAME	*Corydalis aurea* Willd.
FAMILY	Fumitory
RANGE	Pennsylvania to Alaska and south to northern Mexico

33 · Bladderpod

As early as February, the ground between creosote bushes begins to turn yellow as masses of bladderpod start to bloom. The fruits—small spheres that pop if pressed between your thumb and forefinger—give the plant its common name. Seeds of bladderpod contain a unique oil that has been extensively investigated as a potential raw material in the manufacture of rubber, plastics, linoleum, and nylon. If you examine a bladderpod flower, you'll be able to see the crosslike arrangement of petals typical of the crucifer family. The Latin name of the family—Cruciferae—means cross-bearing. Bladderpod is one of a dozen crucifers that herald the arrival of spring in the desert.

Rick and Nora Bowers

SCIENTIFIC NAME	*Lesquerella gordonii* (Gray) S. Wats
FAMILY	Crucifer
RANGE	Oklahoma to Utah, Arizona, California, and northern Mexico

34 · Velvet Mesquite

It is almost impossible to imagine the native peoples of the Southwest without mesquite. For centuries the mesquite provided them with food, fuel, shelter, weapons, tools, fiber, dye, cosmetics, and medicine. These days the mesquite is seen, by ranchers at least, less as a boon than a pest. Since the turn of the century, mesquite has spread from desert washes into the grasslands, making the range less valuable for livestock grazing. Ironically, cattle themselves are partly responsible for the spread of mesquite, since they eat the pods and pass the seeds unharmed

Janice Bowers

through their digestive tracts. Mesquite trees are deciduous; they leaf out in the spring once the danger of frost is well past. Flowers appear in May and occasionally again in August. A characteristic tree of the desert Southwest, velvet mesquite is common in southern Arizona and northern Mexico. A close relative, honey mesquite [*Prosopis glandulosa* Torr. var. *torreyana* (L. Benson) M. C. Johnston], grows in southeastern California, southeastern Arizona, New Mexico, and Texas.

SCIENTIFIC NAME	*Prosopis velutina* Woot.
FAMILY	Pea
RANGE	Southern Arizona and northern Mexico

35 · White Thorn

Janice Bowers

Little yellow balls of fluff, the sweetly scented flowers of white thorn—an acacia—appear in spring and again in summer, depending on the rains. White thorn leaves are divided like fern fronds into fine segments. During dry seasons, most or all of the leaves fall off, then new ones appear following rainy periods lasting several days or more. Acacias are largely tropical and subtropical in their distribution. Many are sensitive to cold, which is one reason the sixty species of acacia in Mexico dwindle to seven in the Southwest and disappear entirely to the north. White thorn is commonly found on rocky or gravelly slopes.

SCIENTIFIC NAME	*Acacia constricta* Benth.
FAMILY	Pea
RANGE	Texas to Arizona and northern Mexico

36 · Desert Senna

Most of the several hundred species of senna grow in the tropics, but a few stragglers, including desert senna, are abundant in our subtropical deserts. Desert senna blooms after winter and summer rains. Unlike many wildflowers that offer both pollen and nectar to insect visitors, desert senna provides only pollen. Bees, the most important pollinators of desert senna flowers, must learn a special technique to harvest the pollen. Since the anthers don't open longitudinally, as do the anthers of most flowers, but by small, apical pores, bees cannot scrape out the pollen. Instead, the bee must wrap its body around an anther and vibrate its flight muscles, thus shaking the pollen out through the pores. Desert senna grows at roadsides and on rocky slopes. A close relative, Bauhin senna [*Senna bauhinioides* (Gray) Irwin & Barneby], resembles desert senna, but has only one pair of leaflets per leaf rather than several.

Rick and Nora Bowers

SCIENTIFIC NAME	*Senna covesii* (Gray) Irwin & Barneby
FAMILY	Pea
RANGE	Arizona, New Mexico, Nevada, California, and northwestern New Mexico

37 · Blue Paloverde

Paloverde, which means "green stick" in Spanish, is well named, because the green trunk, green branches, and green twigs are the first thing you notice about the tree. The small, inconspicuous leaves appear following winter rains, then fall off once the soil dries out late in the spring. Although most plants depend on their leaves to manufacture the sugars needed for growth, the bark has taken over the sugar-making functions for blue paloverde. In April, the trees are covered with a mass of yellow blossoms—one of the most breathtaking sights the desert has to offer. Blue paloverde is common along washes.

C. Allan Morgan

SCIENTIFIC NAME	*Parkinsonia florida* (Benth. ex Gray) S. Wats.
FAMILY	Pea
RANGE	Southeastern California, Arizona, and Sonora

38 · Yellow Paloverde

Although yellow paloverde, also called foothill paloverde or little-leaf paloverde, closely resembles blue paloverde, it isn't too difficult to tell them apart. For one thing, blue paloverde usually grows along washes, whereas yellow paloverde is most common on rocky slopes. For another, the bark of blue paloverde has a distinctly bluish cast, while that of yellow paloverde is yellow-green in hue. The branching pattern of the two trees differs too: the twigs of blue paloverde are long and unbranched, while yellow paloverde has short, intricately branched twigs with thorny tips. In southern Arizona and northern Mexico, yellow paloverde blooms about a month later than blue paloverde, often turning the landscape yellow as every tree bursts into flower at once.

Janice Bowers

SCIENTIFIC NAME	*Parkinsonia microphylla* Torr.
FAMILY	Pea
RANGE	Southeastern California to Arizona, Sonora, and Baja California

39 · Hairy Deer Vetch

C. Allan Morgan

SCIENTIFIC NAME	*Lotus humistratus* Greene
FAMILY	Pea
RANGE	Southern Oregon, California, Nevada, and Arizona to western New Mexico

Hairy deer vetch is one of the "belly flowers" that you must stretch out prone to appreciate. Several species of deer vetch, all ephemerals, grow in the desert. One of the most common is the hairy deer vetch, which forms mats at roadsides, on flats, and in washes. Flowering starts in March and April and ends with the coming of drought and heat in the late spring.

40 · Creosote Bush

One of the most abundant and wide-spread shrubs of the southwestern deserts, creosote bush is admirably suited to its arid habitat. Even when the soil is so dry that other plants become dormant, creosote bush can continue to manufacture the sugars needed for growth. The pungent odor of creosote bush after rain, a familiar one to desert dwellers, comes from the resins on the leaves and young stems. Because of their resinous coat, the leaves resist water loss. During prolonged

C. Allan Morgan

dry spells, they simply fall off, another water-saving strategy. When rainfall recharges soil moisture, creosote responds by putting out new leaves and flower buds. Bees are the most important pollinators of creosote bush flowers. Of the 100 species of bees that frequent the blossoms, twenty-two depend exclusively on the pollen and nectar of creosote bush. Most of these specialist bees nest underground, and the same cool-season rains that trigger the spring blooming of creosote bush also trigger the emergence of the bees. The fluffy white fruits of creosote bush are sectioned like an orange, and each of the five sections contains seven to nine seeds.

SCIENTIFIC NAME	*Larrea tridentata* (Sessé & Moc. ex DC.) Coville
FAMILY	Caltrop
RANGE	Southern California to western Texas

41 · Coulter Hibiscus

SCIENTIFIC NAME	*Hibiscus coulteri* Harvey ex Gray
FAMILY	Mallow Family
RANGE	Eastern Arizona to western Texas

C. Allan Morgan

The large, yellow, cup-shaped flowers of Coulter hibiscus are borne on slender, woody stems several feet above the ground. Coulter hibiscus was named in honor of Thomas Coulter, an Irish botanist who left the Old World in 1824. For several years Coulter collected plants in Mexico, then made his way north to Monterey, California. Eventually he crossed the Mojave Desert to the mouth of the Gila River in western Arizona, becoming the first botanist to collect in the arid regions of southeastern California. Finally, after ten years of wandering and collecting, he departed for England, taking with him a collection of more than 50,000 plant specimens, various botanical notes, and the journal of his excursions. Unfortunately, his notes and journal were lost on the trip from London to Dublin. Broken in health by his travels and disheartened by his loss, he devoted the remaining nine years of his life to setting his collections in order. It wasn't until many years after his death that the importance of Coulter's New World collections was finally recognized.

42 · Desert Blazing Star

Desert blazing star appears to have ten petals—although it actually has only five—because the outermost row of stamens mimics the petals in size, shape, and color. These outermost stamens contain no pollen; their only function, presumably, is to make the blossoms more attractive to potential pollinators. The flowers open in the late afternoon and close around sunset, an unusual schedule that seems to encourage bees (which have a well-developed sense of time) to visit them on a regular basis. In fact, several species of solitary bees synchronize their daily activities with the blooming of desert blazing star. Certain other species of blazing star bloom at night and are pollinated by moths. Desert blazing star is common along roadsides and in sandy places.

Janice Bowers

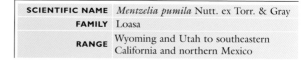

SCIENTIFIC NAME	*Mentzelia pumila* Nutt. ex Torr. & Gray
FAMILY	Loasa
RANGE	Wyoming and Utah to southeastern California and northern Mexico

43 · Engelmann Prickly Pear

Larry Ulrich

Engelmann prickly pear blooms dependably every spring, even in years when winter rainfall has been so far below normal that no spring annuals make an appearance. The yellow flowers turn peach-colored with age and are visited by bees and beetles. Touch the stamens of a prickly pear flower and watch them twist and curl inward. This movement is thought to be a mechanism for dumping more pollen on the bees, thus making pollination more efficient. By August, the ripe, maroon fruits—the prickly pears of the common name—are falling to the hungry mouths of javelina, packrats, and coyotes. Javelina depend year-round on prickly pear pads for food and moisture. Although the high oxalic acid content of the pads makes them poisonous to most animals, javelina have evolved a special kidney modification that allows them to excrete oxalic acid, and they can eat vast quantities of the pads, spines and all, without harm.

SCIENTIFIC NAME	*Opuntia engelmannii* Salm-Dyck ex Engelm. var. *engelmannii*
FAMILY	Cactus
RANGE	New Mexico and southern Utah to southeastern California and adjacent Mexico

44 · Spring Evening Primrose

An early spring wildflower, this evening primrose sometimes blooms even before the last frost of winter. The pale yellow flowers open at dusk and crumple soon after the morning sun touches them. Hawkmoths are probably the only pollinators of the flowers, since no bees in our area have tongues long enough to reach the nectar in the slender floral tubes. Pollen of evening primroses hangs together in sticky threads that cling to the fuzzy bodies of the moths, which then transfer pollen from one plant to another. Spring evening primrose grows on rocky slopes and gravelly flats.

Randy Prentice

SCIENTIFIC NAME	*Oenothera primiveris* Gray
FAMILY	Evening Primrose
RANGE	Texas to Nevada and California

45 · Yellow Linanthus

SCIENTIFIC NAME	*Linanthus aureus* (Nutt.) J.M. Porter & L.A. Johnson ssp. *aureus*
FAMILY	Linanthus Phlox
RANGE	Western Texas to southern Nevada and southeastern Utah

The flowers of yellow linanthus dwarf its threadlike stems and tiny leaves. After wet winters the diminutive plants sometimes cover gravelly flats with yellow blossoms. In western Arizona and southern California, a variety that has white flowers instead of yellow grows in sandy soils. Yellow linanthus is one of a handful of spring wildflowers that creep from the desert into desert grassland and oak woodland.

Steven P. McLaughlin

46 · Fiddleneck

Bruce Griffin

The common name fiddleneck comes from the stems, which are curved like the scroll of a violin. This kind of flowering stalk, called a scorpioid inflorescence because it resembles a scorpion's tail, is characteristic of plants in the borage family. The bristly hairs on the leaves and stems are also characteristic of borages, at least of those that grow in the desert. Fiddleneck can be abundant along roadsides, in old fields, and in other disturbed spots. It blooms in the spring.

SCIENTIFIC NAME	*Amsinckia menziesii* (Lehm.) A. Nels. & J.F. Macbr. var. *intermedia* (Fisch & C.A. Mey.)
FAMILY	Borage
RANGE	Western New Mexico to California

47 · Unicorn Plant

If, as you walk through the desert, you feel something wrap around your ankle, relax: it's probably just a devil's claw, the seed pod of the unicorn plant. The green pod is shaped like a sickle, but when it matures, the long beak splits in half, making two curved arms like shepherd's crooks. These hook onto any convenient passerby, thus dispersing the seeds. Once summer rains have moistened the soil, the unicorn plant puts out yellow, five-lobed flowers and broad, almost circular leaves. Its blossoms are pollinated by a solitary bee (*Perdita hurdi*) that snips a small hole in the bottom of the flower tube before the flowers open. Once the bee has gathered a full load of pollen, she flies immediately to an open flower to collect nectar. Since only closed unicorn plant flowers provide pollen, and only open ones supply nectar, the bee cross-pollinates the blossoms in fulfilling both her needs. Unicorn plant grows along roadsides and in washes.

C. Allan Morgan

SCIENTIFIC NAME	*Proboscidea althaeifolia* (Benth.) Decne.
FAMILY	Sesame
RANGE	Texas to southeastern California and northern Mexico

48 · Coyote Gourd

Steven P. McLaughlin

SCIENTIFIC NAME	*Cucurbita digitata* Gray
FAMILY	Gourd
RANGE	Southwestern New Mexico to southeastern California and northern Mexico

Yellow balls dangling like Christmas tree decorations in mesquite trees are coyote gourds, a close relative of our cultivated squashes. Coyote gourd vines snake across the ground or climb fences and trees. Their large, floppy, yellow flowers look much like squash flowers, but the similarity stops there. Whereas garden squashes have been carefully bred to be fleshy and flavorful, wild squashes are extremely bitter and can be toxic in large quantities. Coyote gourd flowers, like those of most squashes, open early in the morning, sometimes before dawn. Even so, the squash and gourd bees, which rely exclusively on the pollen and nectar of wild gourds, are up in time to pollinate the flowers. Coyote gourd blooms from summer to fall.

49 · Common Sunflower

The sunflower family, the largest plant family in the world with about 20,000 species, is named after the common sunflower, which grows in ditches, along roadsides, and in fields throughout the West. The common sunflower has a venerable history. Long before the time of Spanish contact, Hopi Indians in northern Arizona had domesticated a large-headed variety with purple-shelled achenes. The Indians ate the seeds and soaked the purple shells in water to make a dye for decorating baskets and bodies. Spaniards took the seeds to Europe, and, after some time, sunflowers arrived in Russia, where they were bred for larger

Janice Bowers

SCIENTIFIC NAME	*Helianthus annuus* L.
FAMILY	Sunflower
RANGE	Throughout the West

seeds and higher oil content. Eventually this Mammoth Russian variety was introduced into the United States, bringing the sunflower full circle.

50 · Dune Sunflower

SCIENTIFIC NAME	*Helianthus niveus* (Benth.) Brandeg. ssp. *tephrodes* (Gray) Heiser
FAMILY	Sunflower
RANGE	Southeastern California and northwestern Sonora

Janice Bowers

Dune sunflower, a close relative of the common sunflower, grows only on deep sand in southeastern California and northwestern Sonora. Whereas the common sunflower has green and raspy leaves, a dense coat of hairs makes leaves of dune sunflower velvety and white. The roots of common sunflower grow straight down into the soil, but those of dune sunflower radiate from the plant for many yards. The velvety leaves and vinelike roots of dune sunflower are important adaptations to its hot, bright, mobile habitat. Velvety hairs keep the leaves from losing too much water and from becoming too hot; elongated roots anchor the plant so that it won't be uprooted by shifting sands. Dune sunflower blooms in the spring and sometimes again in the fall.

51 · Desert Sunflower

Rick and Nora Bowers

SCIENTIFIC NAME	*Geraea canescens* Torr. & Gray
FAMILY	Sunflower
RANGE	Southwestern Arizona and southeastern California

One of the earliest spring wildflowers in the low deserts of southwestern Arizona and southeastern California, desert sunflower starts to bloom in February. Desert sunflower seeds require about an inch of rain to germinate, as do the seeds of many desert wildflowers. One species of solitary bee that depends solely on desert sunflower for pollen times its emergence from underground burrows to coincide with the blooming of desert sunflower. The same climatic signals that trigger germination and flowering of the desert sunflower probably also cue the bees.

52 · Hierba Amarilla

SCIENTIFIC NAME	*Hymenothrix wislizeni* Gray
FAMILY	Sunflower
RANGE	Southern Arizona, New Mexico, and northern Mexico

Janice Bowers

Hierba amarilla, an annual often abundant along roadsides and in washes in the late summer and fall, superficially resembles a goldenrod, but the flower clusters of hierba amarilla are much looser. Also, no goldenrod in the Southwest has the deeply cut leaves of hierba amarilla. Its scientific name, *Hymenothrix wislizeni,* commemorates Friedrich Adolph Wislizenus, a native of Germany who came to the U.S. in 1835 at the age of twenty-five. After practicing medicine in St. Louis, he joined a party of U.S. troops who were traveling to Santa Fe just before the end of the war with Mexico. Perhaps foolishly, Wislizenus entered Chihuahua and was promptly captured by the Mexicans. While a prisoner of war, he was allowed to collect plants in the local area and in doing so discovered a number of new species, including hierba amarilla.

53 · Brittlebush

The brittlebush, named for its stems, which snap easily between thumb and forefinger, is also called *incienso,* after the golden sap once used as incense in Mexican churches. When the soil is cool and moist, the leaves are pale green and absorb as much sunlight as possible. When the soil turns hot and dry in the summertime, a new set of leaves with a velvety coat of white hairs appears. The dense hairs block out some of the sun's rays and keep the leaves from becoming too hot to manufacture the sugars needed for growth. This windowshade effect is one reason brittlebush is so successful in the hottest, driest parts of the desert. A spring-flowering perennial, it grows on rocky slopes and gravelly plains.

Bruce Griffin

SCIENTIFIC NAME	*Encelia farinosa* Gray ex Torr.
FAMILY	Sunflower
RANGE	Southern Nevada, Arizona, southern California, and northwestern Mexico

54 · Paperdaisy

Paperdaisy gets its name from the ray flowers, which turn papery and persist long after they have lost their bright yellow color. At its best, paperdaisy forms compact, hemispherical mounds of yellow blossoms. The main blooming period occurs in the spring, but if summer rains have been good, the plants will flower again in August and September. Paperdaisy often colonizes disturbed areas such as abandoned dirt roads.

C. Allan Morgan

SCIENTIFIC NAME	*Psilostrophe cooperi* (Gray) Greene
FAMILY	Sunflower
RANGE	Southeastern California to Utah, New Mexico, and northern Mexico

55 · Desert Marigold

Larry Ulrich

Desert marigold blooms sporadically throughout the year, even in the winter when little else is in flower. A common roadside plant, desert marigold is also an important colonizer of disturbed ground and can often be found on dirt roads and pipelines. Like the flowers of paperdaisy, those of desert marigold turn papery with age. Although the two often grow together and bloom at the same time, it's easy to tell them apart. Paperdaisy has small leaves along the entire length of the stem, whereas the leaves of desert marigold are mostly clustered near the base of the stem.

SCIENTIFIC NAME	*Baileya multiradiata* Harvey & Gray ex Gray
FAMILY	Sunflower
RANGE	West Texas and Chihuahua to Utah and southeastern California

56 · Sweetbush

Steven P. McLaughlin

A rounded shrub to three feet tall, sweetbush lacks leaves much of the year. Each flower head contains several dozen disk flowers, no rays. The sweetly scented heads are particularly attractive to butterflies. One desert butterfly, the Wright metalmark (*Calephelis wrighti*), lays its eggs on the leafless stems, and the developing caterpillars, lacking leaves to feed on, eat the outer layer of stem tissue. Sweetbush blooms from spring to fall along roadsides and in washes.

SCIENTIFIC NAME	*Bebbia juncea* (Benth.) Greene
FAMILY	Sunflower
RANGE	Western Texas to southern Nevada, southern California, and northern Mexico

Randy Prentice

The genus *Senecio* is among the largest in the sunflower family: between 2,000 and 3,000 species of *Senecio* are known to science. The name *Senecio,* which comes from the Latin word *senex,* meaning "old man," refers to the soft, white fluff on the ripe seeds. Many species of *Senecio* are commonly called groundsel or ragwort. The desert groundsel is a common spring flower and often grows in washes and roadside ditches.

SCIENTIFIC NAME	*Senecio flaccidus* Less. var. *monoensis* (E. Greene) B. Turner & T. Barkley
FAMILY	Sunflower
RANGE	Southeastern California to Utah and Arizona

SCIENTIFIC NAME	*Trixis californica* Kellogg
FAMILY	Sunflower
RANGE	Western Texas to southern California and northern Mexico

A low shrub with bright green leaves, trixis grows on bouldered slopes or along washes, often in the shade of trees. The flower heads of trixis each contain about a dozen yellow flowers. Individual flowers are two-lipped: one lip is like a small ray and has three teeth, the other is simply a pair of lobes. This strange flower seems to be halfway between the ray flower and the disk flower of the common sunflower, sharing attributes of both. The genus name *Trixis* comes from a Greek word meaning threefold and refers to the three-lobed lip of the flower. Trixis blooms in spring and fall.

Rick and Nora Bowers

59 · Desert Mariposa

C. Allan Morgan

SCIENTIFIC NAME	*Calochortus kennedyi* Porter
FAMILY	Lily
RANGE	Southeastern California to Arizona and northern Sonora

You won't see the desert mariposa—a wild lily—every spring; only in years when some crucial factor has been met do the silky, vermilion flowers appear en masse on rocky slopes. During other years the bulbs stay hidden underground, waiting for the right combination of temperature and rainfall before they'll send up leaves and flower stalks. Each of the three petals of the desert mariposa bears a large, dark spot at the base. This spot, called the gland, is characteristic of mariposa lilies and varies in shape, color, and hairiness from one species to another. So distinctive are the glands that an expert can identify some of the fifty-seven species of mariposa lily by a single petal.

60 · Mexican Poppy

Mexican poppy is a good example of how species evolve. Twenty thousand years ago, when the climate of the Southwest was cool and wet, California poppy (*Eschscholzia californica* Cham. subsp. *californica*) probably grew from Arizona to coastal California. Starting about 8,000 years ago, as the regional climate became more arid, poppies in what is now Arizona became adapted to the hotter, drier conditions of the developing desert. Mexican poppy hasn't differentiated from California poppy quite enough to be considered a separate species, and most botanists agree that the Mexican poppy is a subspecies of the California poppy.

C. Allan Morgan

Mexican poppy, like its California relative, blooms in the spring. Its four petals and spring-flowering habit distinguish it from the five-petaled summer poppy, which usually blooms following summer rains.

SCIENTIFIC NAME	*Eschscholzia californica* Cham. ssp. *mexicana* (Greene) C. Clark
FAMILY	Poppy
RANGE	West Texas to southern Utah, southeastern California, and northern Sonora

61 · Summer Poppy

SCIENTIFIC NAME	*Kallstroemia grandiflora* Torr. ex Gray
FAMILY	Caltrop
RANGE	Texas to Arizona and Mexico

Summer poppy, also called Arizona poppy, isn't a poppy at all, although it certainly resembles the Mexican poppy that blooms in the spring. Actually, summer poppy is related to creosote bush. Summer poppy seeds germinate in response to summer rains and complete their life cycle in a few months. By the time the soil has dried out completely, the summer poppies have died, leaving seeds to endure until conditions are right once again. Since germination inhibitors coat the seeds, they won't germinate until every trace of the inhibiting chemical has washed away, a process that usually takes several seasons. The orange flowers with their dark vermilion centers attract a variety of insect visitors.

Randy Prentice

62 · Apricot Mallow

Several species of globe mallow are common in the desert. Most have scalloped leaves and peachy-pink flowers. Coulter globe mallow [*Sphaeralcea coulteri* (S. Wats.) Gray] is a spring-flowering annual of sandy soils. Caliche globe mallow (*Sphaeralcea laxa* Woot. & Standl.) is common on limestone and on rocky soils cemented with caliche. Apricot mallow, the most drought-tolerant of the three, can be found on rocky slopes and along roadsides. The large, apricot-colored petals—the largest in the genus—and the thick, whitish leaves set apricot mallow apart from the other desert globe mallows.

Randy Prentice

SCIENTIFIC NAME	*Sphaeralcea ambigua* Gray
FAMILY	Mallow
RANGE	Southeastern Utah to California, Sonora, and northern Baja California

63 · Barrel Cactus

According to legend, the barrel cactus is practically a drinking fountain for thirsty travelers. The reality is a bit different. To get water from a barrel cactus, you would have to cut off the top of the plant, then pound the flesh inside to a moist pulp. According to some, the taste of barrel cactus juice is insipid; others find it astringent. One species supposedly tastes like watermelon, another is said to be slimy. In any case, cacti are protected by law in Arizona, California, and New Mexico, and it is illegal to dig up or mutilate them. The prudent desert traveler carries his or her own supply of water. A nonconformist in the cactus world, barrel cactus blooms in late summer instead of in the spring like most southwestern cacti. The flowers, which vary from yellow to orange to red, grow in successive wreaths on the crown of the plant. The yellow fruits are relished by rodents, birds, and javelina.

Bruce Griffin

SCIENTIFIC NAME	*Ferocactus wislizeni* (Engelm.) Britt. & Rose
FAMILY	Cactus
RANGE	Western Texas to Arizona and northern Mexico

64 · Staghorn Cholla

Versicolor, the species name of staghorn cholla, means variously colored. It could refer either to the slender stems, which turn red with drought or cold, or to the flowers, which are brick red on some plants, brassy yellow on others. The staghorn cholla is one of the largest of the southwestern chollas, sometimes reaching a height of six feet. Like many of the prickly pears, staghorn cholla blooms late in the spring after winter rains have ceased and before the summer rains have begun. Certain ants collect nectar from special glands on cholla buds and joints, just as they will visit your sugar bowl, should they discover it. Staghorn cholla is common on plains, rocky slopes, and canyon bottoms.

C. Allan Morgan

SCIENTIFIC NAME	*Cylindropuntia versicolor* (Engelm. ex Coult.) F.M. Knuth
FAMILY	Cactus
RANGE	Southern Arizona and northern Mexico

65 · Ocotillo

The long, wandlike stems of ocotillo are a familiar sight in the western deserts. Each ocotillo plant is a sensitive barometer of soil moisture. When the soil is dry, the stems are leafless, gray, and thorny. Once rains have recharged the soil, every ocotillo stem sprouts a green, leafy sheath that lasts just until the soil dries out again. This cycle of leafiness and nudity can happen a half-dozen times or more during the year, depending on rainfall. Ocotillos usually flower between March and May in time for the northward migration of hummingbirds. The waxy, red, tubular flowers attract not only hummingbirds but carpenter bees, house finches, and many other birds and insects.

Randy Prentice

SCIENTIFIC NAME	*Fouquieria splendens* Engelm.
FAMILY	Ocotillo
RANGE	Arizona, California, and northern Mexico

66 · Indian Paintbrush

Even expert botanists have difficulty in telling apart the 200 species of Indian paintbrush in western North America. Indian paintbrush flowers are inconspicuous: it is the bright red bracts beneath each flower that catch the eye. Most, if not all, species of Indian paintbrush are hemiparasitic, depending on host plants to supply water and nutrients. Indian paintbrush seedlings grow poorly or won't grow at all if the plants fail to find a host. Like most hemiparasites, even fully grown plants of Indian paintbrush lack a well-developed root system. The underground portion of the plant consists of special conducting tubes, called haustoria, that attach to the roots of the host—often oaks or grasses in the Southwest. The figwort family contains many hemiparasites, including owl's clover.

Larry Ulrich

SCIENTIFIC NAME	*Castilleja* sp.
FAMILY	Figwort
RANGE	Western North America

67 · Desert Honeysuckle

Desert honeysuckle belongs to the acanthus family, a largely tropical group with a dozen or so representatives in the warmer parts of the Southwest. Hummingbirds pollinate the flowers, which bloom during the spring migratory season. Each of the several seeds inside the pod is held by a hook; when the ripe capsule splits open, the hook curls upwards, flinging the seed into the air. *Anisacanthus thurberi,* the scientific name of desert honeysuckle, commemorates George Thurber, a nineteenth-century pharmacist who eventually became a botanist. This move was less unusual then than it may seem now. In those days, plants were an important source of drugs, and pharmacists were by necessity botanists. Thurber served as botanist on the United States and Mexico boundary survey from 1850 to 1853 and made a large collection of southwestern plants that added much to botanical knowledge. A shrub to five feet tall, desert honeysuckle grows in sandy washes.

Rick and Nora Bowers

SCIENTIFIC NAME	*Anisacanthus thurberi* (Torr.) Gray
FAMILY	Acanthus
RANGE	Southwestern New Mexico to Arizona and northern Mexico

68 · Chuparosa

Find a desert wash where chuparosa blooms bountifully in the early spring and you will almost certainly see one or more species of hummingbirds busily probing the red, tubular flowers. The northward migration of hummingbirds from southern Mexico seems to be timed so that the birds arrive in the desert just as the chuparosa starts to bloom in February. As a bird hovers at a blossom, the protruding stamens brush its head, leaving a golden smudge of pollen. Chuparosa and desert honeysuckle, both members of the acanthus family, bear a superficial resemblance to one another but can be easily distinguished: stems of chuparosa are soft and covered with velvety hairs, whereas those of desert honeysuckle are woody and have shreddy bark; leaves of chuparosa are broad and triangular, those of desert honeysuckle narrow and elliptical; and flowers of chuparosa are bright red, those of desert honeysuckle vermillion or even orange. Chuparosa grows in washes.

Randy Prentice

SCIENTIFIC NAME	*Justicia californica* (Benth.) D. Gibson
FAMILY	Acanthus
RANGE	Southeastern California and southwestern Arizona to northwestern Sonora and northern Baja California

Common in gravel along roads and on dry slopes, trailing four o'clock blooms sporadically from April to October. The hot pink to magenta blossoms vary from the size of a shirt button to the size of a quarter. Each scalloped blossom is really three flowers in one. In spite of their common name, the flowers of trailing four o'clock open around sunrise and close about midday, unless it's cloudy, when they may stay open all day long. Butterflies and bees visit the flowers for the nectar that accumulates in the short tubes. If no insects come, the flowers can pollinate themselves, as can many desert annuals.

Randy Prentice

SCIENTIFIC NAME	*Allionia incarnata* L.
FAMILY	Four O'Clock
RANGE	Colorado and Utah to southern Mexico

Sand verbena, a plant of dunes and sandy flats, often makes a calico patchwork with dune evening primrose, woody bottle washer, spectacle pod, and other sand-loving wildflowers. The long tubes of the sweetly scented, magenta flowers ensure that only insects with correspondingly long tongues—mainly butterflies and moths—can reach the nectar inside. The broad wings of the seed pods catch readily in the wind, blowing the seeds from one dune field to another. Sand verbena can be found in southeastern California and southwestern Arizona and adjacent northern Mexico. A different sand verbena grows on the coastal dunes in California, Baja California, and Sonora and yet another grows at White Sands National Monument in southern New Mexico.

Janice Bowers

SCIENTIFIC NAME	*Abronia villosa* S. Wats.
FAMILY	Four O'Clock
RANGE	Southeastern California and southwestern Arizona and adjacent northern Mexico

71 · Fairy Duster

The fairy duster, *Calliandra eriophylla,* is a small shrub most noticeable in the spring when covered with pale pink to deep rose flowers. The petals of the fairy duster are inconspicuous: it is the long, pink filaments of the stamens that make the showy display. In fact, *Calliandra* means "beautiful stamen." Fairy duster pollen comes in teardrop-shaped packets that adhere to the bodies of insect visitors, mainly butterflies. When butterflies visit one fairy duster plant after another, they transfer the pollen packets, thus pollinating the flowers. Fairy duster grows in washes at the arid, western edge of its range in southeastern California. In southern Arizona and west Texas, it thrives on rocky slopes of mountain foothills.

C. Allan Morgan

SCIENTIFIC NAME	*Calliandra eriophylla* Benth.
FAMILY	Pea
RANGE	Southeastern California, southern Arizona, and western Texas

72 · Arizona Lupine

Most of the 100 species of lupines in North America bear characteristic bee-pollinated flowers: the large, uppermost petal, called the banner, catches the bee's attention; the two wing petals at either side of the banner provide a landing spot for the bee; and the two petals inside the wings enclose and protect the stamens and pistil in a boat-shaped arrangement called the keel. Only a strong insect, such as a bumblebee, can force the wing petals downwards to gain access to the pollen and nectar inside the keel. The creamy splotch on the banner of every Arizona lupine flower is a nectar guide that directs the bee to the reward inside. Once a flower has been pollinated, the nectar guide changes from cream-colored to red-violet, alerting bees not to waste time on that particular blossom. In years of plentiful winter rainfall, Arizona lupine makes magenta rivers along roadsides and in washes.

Janice Bowers

SCIENTIFIC NAME	*Lupinus arizonicus* (S. Wats.) S. Wats.
FAMILY	Pea
RANGE	Southern Nevada, southeastern California, southwestern Arizona, and adjacent Mexico

73 · Ironwood

When ironwood blooms, entire trees can be covered with the pink, sweet-pea-shaped flowers, and the canopies become alive with bumblebees, carpenter bees, honeybees, and hummingbirds. Ironwoods tend to drop many leaves just before they bloom; this strategy enables them to divert sugars from the leaves to the flowers and developing fruits. The wood, as its name implies, is extremely hard, and it takes many years for dead ironwood trees to decay. Seri Indians of coastal Sonora carve animal figures from ironwood. Ironwood grows mostly in desert washes.

Bruce Griffin

SCIENTIFIC NAME	*Olneya tesota* Gray
FAMILY	Pea
RANGE	Southeastern California, Arizona, Sonora, and Baja California

74 · Southern Freckled Milkvetch

SCIENTIFIC NAME	*Astragalus lentiginosus* Dougl. var. *australis* Barneby
FAMILY	Pea
RANGE	Southern Arizona to southwestern New Mexico and adjacent Mexico

It's easy to recognize a milkvetch—also called locoweed—but hard to tell which of the 400 species of milkvetch it is. The characteristics of the pods are important in telling the various milkvetches apart. In some, the pods are so thin you can see the seeds inside; in others the pods are tough and woody. Some species have inflated pods; in others they are flat and sickle-shaped. The freckled milkvetch is one of the most widely distributed of the milkvetches: its thirty-nine varieties occur from Washington to Chihuahua and from sea level to the alpine zone. Southern freckled milkvetch, the common variety in the Sonoran Desert, blooms in the spring. It can be recognized by the sprawling habit of the plants, the pink-purple flowers, and the inflated, papery pods.

Janice Bowers

75 · Range Ratany

Most of the year, range ratany is an inconspicuous shrub with gray, rigid branches and small,
furry leaves. When it blooms following winter
and summer rains, however, the heavy load of
red-violet flowers and fat, spiny seed pods
make it hard to overlook. Female bees of the
genus *Centris* are the sole pollinators of range
ratany. Unlike most flowers, which offer nectar
to pollinators, range ratany provides oil
instead. *Centris* bees mix the oil with pollen
from other plants, then use the oil-pollen paste
to provision their larvae.

C. Allan Morgan

SCIENTIFIC NAME	*Krameria erecta* Willd. ex J.A. Schultes
FAMILY	Krameria
RANGE	Western Texas to southern Nevada, Arizona, southern California, and northern Mexico

76 · Filaree

Filaree, also called heron-bill, is one of
the earliest wildflowers to bloom in the
spring and often colors acres of desert a
delicate lavender. A native of Europe,
filaree was introduced into California in
the eighteenth century by the
Spaniards. Eventually its seeds came to
Arizona on the woolly backs and legs of
sheep. Nowadays, filaree flourishes
throughout the Southwest from desert
to pine forest. Filaree seeds literally
plant themselves. The distinctive fruits,
shaped like miniature swords when

C. Allan Morgan

green, curl into corkscrews as they ripen. When rainfall moistens these
corkscrews, they uncurl, and the spiraling motion drives the tips of the fruits
into the ground.

SCIENTIFIC NAME	*Erodium cicutarium* (L.) L'Hér. ex Ait.
FAMILY	Geranium
RANGE	Throughout the United States

77 · Desert Hibiscus

SCIENTIFIC NAME	*Hibiscus denudatus* Benth.
FAMILY	Mallow
RANGE	Western Texas to southern California and northern Mexico

Steve P. McLaughlin

We usually think of hibiscus as a tropical plant, and most of the 300 species of hibiscus are indeed native to tropical and subtropical regions. A few, desert hibiscus among them, creep from the tropics into the arid parts of the Southwest. The small, fuzzy leaves of desert hibiscus are a water-saving adaptation to the desert environment, as is their habit of falling during periods of drought. Inside the pink or lavender cup of a desert hibiscus flower stands the brushlike column of stamens and stigmas characteristic of the mallow family. Desert hibiscus blooms in spring and again in summer and can be found in shallow washes and on rocky slopes.

78 · Jumping Cholla

One botanist has said that, from a distance, a jumping cholla looks like a haystack on a post because of the dense, straw-colored spines. These same spines hook so readily to any passerby that the joints sometimes seem to jump off the plant. Such detached stems often take root and grow into new plants. Because vegetative reproduction is so successful, the plants rely but little on sexual reproduction, and the plump fruits usually contain only sterile seeds. The magenta to pale pink flowers appear from May to August. Jumping cholla is common on plains and gentle slopes.

C. Allan Morgan

SCIENTIFIC NAME	*Cylindropuntia fulgida* (Engelm.) F.M. Knuth
FAMILY	Cactus
RANGE	Southern Arizona and New Mexico into Sonora and Sinaloa

79 · Strawberry Hedgehog

Bruce Griffin

SCIENTIFIC NAME	*Echinocereus engelmannii* (Parry ex Engelm.) Lem.
FAMILY	Cactus
RANGE	Southern California, Utah, and Nevada to northern Mexico

Strawberry hedgehog, named for the sweet, fleshy fruits that ripen in the summer, comprises sixteen varieties. Many have needlelike, yellow spines all pointing downward. Flowers can be magenta, purple, lavender, or pale pink. The scientific name of strawberry hedgehog—*Echinocereus engelmannii*—commemorates George Engelmann, a German-born botanist and doctor who came to the United States in 1832 at the age of twenty-three and eventually developed a successful obstetrical practice in St. Louis. Like many medical men of the day, he was as much a botanist as he was a doctor. Because his medical practice kept him busy, he had little time for fieldwork and concentrated instead on identifying the collections sent to him by botanical explorers. Today he is best remembered for his work on the cactus family, and it is appropriate that several species of cacti, including *Echinocereus engelmannii*, bear his name.

80 · Pincushion Cactus

Looking closely at this cactus you'll be able to see the tubercules—small, nipplelike protrusions—that cover the stem. These give the plant its scientific name of *Mammillaria*, which comes from *mammila*, the Latin word for nipple. The flowers are small—only an inch or so in diameter—but large for pincushions as a group. Because of their attractive flowers and stems, pincushions are prized as ornamentals, and over 100 species are in cultivation. In the wild, pincushion cactus grows tucked among rocks or half-hidden under large chollas. It usually blooms late in the spring.

C. Allan Morgan

SCIENTIFIC NAME	*Mammillaria grahamii* Engelm.
FAMILY	Cactus
RANGE	California and Arizona

The beavertail is one of about a dozen species of prickly pear cacti in the Southwest. Prickly pear pads are modified stems that serve several functions: water storage, photosynthesis, and flower production. Pads of beavertail look so smooth you might think they have no spines at all, but appearances are deceiving. Though the pads lack the long, straight spines characteristic of most prickly pears, they are abundantly supplied with glochids—miniscule bristles with wickedly barbed tips. A thick layer of wax gives the pads their gray-blue color and helps protect them from desiccation. The flowers bloom as early as February, and by March, the gorgeous magenta flowers decorate many a barren hillside.

Larry Ulrich

SCIENTIFIC NAME	*Opuntia basilaris* Engelm. & Bigelow
FAMILY	Cactus
RANGE	Southeastern California and western Arizona

Like many desert wildflowers, purplemat accommodates itself to the weather. In years of plentiful winter rainfall, the radiating stems bear scores of small, bell-shaped flowers in the spring. When rains have been poor, however, a single flower might constitute the entire plant. In this way, plants can set seed and perpetuate the species even in unfavorable years. Purplemat is an ephemeral, which means that it lives for just six to eight weeks. We could call such wildflowers annuals instead of ephemerals, but "annual" implies a plant that lasts as long as the growing season. In the desert, where the growing season—the period free of frost—is nine or ten months long, annuals in this sense are few. Most desert annuals are actually ephemerals.

Clin: Farlinger

SCIENTIFIC NAME	*Nama demissum* Gray
FAMILY	Waterleaf
RANGE	Southern California to southern Utah and southern Arizona

83 · Parry Beardtongue

SCIENTIFIC NAME	*Penstemon parryi* (Gray) Gray
FAMILY	Figwort
RANGE	Arizona and northern Mexico

Randy Prentice

Penstemon, the genus name of Parry beardtongue, means "five stamens." If you look inside a flower of Parry beardtongue or of any other *Penstemon,* however, you'll see only four stamens. The fifth stamen, called a staminode, has lost its anther. Instead, it has a dense cluster of hairs near the tip. The bearded staminode gives rise to the common name beardtongue for this and many other species of *Penstemon.* Parry beardtongue commemorates Charles Christopher Parry, one of the great plant collectors of the nineteenth century. Although trained as a physician, Parry quickly found his medical duties vexatious, and he drifted from medicine into botany, an easier feat in those days when the distinction between the two fields was not very clear. As botanist on the U.S. and Mexico boundary survey from 1849 to 1851, Parry amassed a large collection of plants from the border region, many of them unknown to science at the time. Parry beardtongue thrives in desert washes, and occasionally the plants are abundant on burned-over slopes in desert grassland.

84 · Owl's Clover

You probably know that a parasite is a plant that robs its host of water, nutrients, and sugar. Owl's clover is a hemiparasite: like a parasite, it attaches itself to the roots of a host plant, robbing it of water and minerals, but, as a green-leaved plant, it manufactures its own food. Often host-parasite relationships are quite specific. One species of mistletoe, for example, grows only on oaks, another only on junipers. Owl's clover, however, will grow on almost any host, although some hosts are more beneficial than others. In Arizona, owl's clover has been found attached to desert larkspur, bladderpod, Mexican poppy, and desert lupine, among others. Owl's clover plants that connect with choice hosts flower earlier and produce more seeds than plants that attach to less desirable hosts or that find no host at all. Like the lupines and poppies with which it often grows, owl's clover can be abundant in good springs.

C. Allan Morgan

SCIENTIFIC NAME	*Castilleja exserta* (Heller) Chuang & Heckard ssp. *exserta*
FAMILY	Figwort
RANGE	California to Arizona, Sonora, and Baja California

85 · Desert Willow

Although the desert willow isn't really a willow, it does grow along streambeds as do true willows. Usually, though, the streambeds where desert willow thrives flow only after heavy rains. The capacious flowers of desert willow just fit the plump bodies of the carpenter bees and bumblebees that pollinate them. Lavender streaks on the orchid-pink blossoms guide the bees to the pool of nectar at the bottom of the flower tube. The stigma of desert willow is sensitive and folds shut a few seconds after a bee touches it. This helps to prevent self-pollination as the bee leaves the flower. Desert willow is a deciduous tree that can grow to twenty-five feet tall. It blooms in the spring and occasionally in the summer.

Rick and Nora Bowers

SCIENTIFIC NAME	*Chilopsis linearis* (Cav.) Sweet
FAMILY	Bignonia
RANGE	Western Texas to southern California and northern Mexico

86 · Wild Hyacinth

Growing on rocky slopes among saguaro, yellow paloverde, and brittlebush, wild hyacinth is one of the common spring wildflowers of the desert. Indians and early settlers ate the bulbs, which grow tightly wedged between rocks. Plants that grow from bulbs are characteristic of Mediterranean climates, where winters are wet and summers are dry. In California, for example, at least 170 species of bulb plants can be found. Only a few species have become adapted to the harsher regime of the desert.

Bruce Griffin

SCIENTIFIC NAME	*Dichelostemma capitatum* (Benth.) Wood ssp. *capitatum*
FAMILY	Lily
RANGE	Southern California to southern New Mexico and northern Sonora

87 · Smoke Tree

From a distance, the gray stems and branches of smoke tree give an impression of smokiness, thus the common name. Only the real desert rats get to see the plant covered with purple flowers, for it blooms in May and June during the hottest, driest time of the year when few people want to be out in the desert. Smoke tree typically grows in washes, usually with such desert trees as ironwood and blue paloverde, also members of the pea family. The small leaves that appear after winter rains last only a short while. The rest of the year, it is the thorny branch tips that carry on the work of photosynthesis—manufacturing the sugars needed for growth.

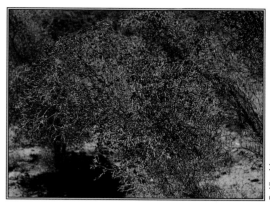

C. Allan Morgan

SCIENTIFIC NAME	*Psorothamnus spinosus* (Gray) Barneby
FAMILY	Pea
RANGE	Arizona, southeastern California, Baja California, and Sonora

88 · Organ Pipe

In Mexico, the organ pipe, a multi-stemmed columnar cactus, occurs as far south as Sinaloa. But because low temperatures check the northward movement of the organ pipe, it enters the United States only in southwestern Arizona, where it encounters only moderate, occasional frost. The pale lavender, musky flowers begin to open about an hour before dark and close by mid-morning of the following day. Sanborn's long-nosed bats, which hover before the flowers to drink the very sweet nectar, are the most important pollinators of the organ pipe cactus in Arizona. Unlike the saguaro, which has spongy rods for its skeleton, each branch of the organ pipe cactus is supported by a hollow wood cylinder. After the cactus dies, its succulent tissue rots away, leaving the wooden skeleton.

C. Allan Morgan

SCIENTIFIC NAME	*Stenocereus thurberi* (Engelm.) Buxbaum
FAMILY	Cactus
RANGE	Southwestern Arizona to Sinaloa

89 · Wild Heliotrope

SCIENTIFIC NAME	*Phacelia bombycina* Woot. & Standl.
FAMILY	Waterleaf
RANGE	Southern Arizona and southeastern New Mexico; related species found in southeastern California and west Texas

One of the most common spring wildflowers in the desert, wild heliotrope flourishes on rocky slopes, along roadsides, and in sandy washes. The lavender to purple flowers grow in tight clusters that are turned under like the scroll of a violin. The foliage has an unpleasant, skunky odor, particularly when crushed. Some people develop a poison-ivy-like allergy to the plants.

Janice Bowers

90 · Desert Verbena

Desert verbena is a typical butterfly-pollinated wildflower. The blossoms are pink to lavender, the favorite colors of butterflies, and the flat-topped flower clusters make a convenient landing platform. The desert verbena, a true verbena, should not be confused with sand verbena, a member of the four o'clock family. It's not hard to tell them apart: desert verbena flowers have short tubes only a fraction of an inch long, whereas those of sand verbena measure nearly an inch in length; desert verbena is perennial, sand verbena annual; and desert verbena stems are square, those of sand verbena round. Blooming in spring and summer, desert verbena can be common on rocky slopes and in roadside ditches.

Rick and Nora Bowers

SCIENTIFIC NAME	*Glandularia gooddingii* (Briq.) Solbrig
FAMILY	Verbena
RANGE	Texas to Utah, California, and northern Mexico

91 · New Mexico Verbena

Steven P. McLaughlin

SCIENTIFIC NAME	*Verbena neomexicana* (Gray) Small
FAMILY	Verbena
RANGE	Texas to southern California and northern Mexico

In contrast to the flat-topped flower clusters of desert verbena, blossoms of New Mexico verbena are arranged one above the other in narrow spikes. The flat-topped arrangement seems to facilitate butterfly pollination, the spike arrangement bee pollination. Even so, butterflies as well as bees visit the small, purple flowers of New Mexico verbena. A perennial herb that flowers in spring and summer, New Mexico verbena grows on rocky slopes and can be abundant on limestone.

92 · Desert Lavender

A shrub of rocky slopes and sandy washes, desert lavender blooms sporadically throughout the year. The small, lavender flowers attract bees and hummingbirds. *Hyptis emoryi*, the scientific name of desert lavender, commemorates William H. Emory, commissioner of the team that surveyed the United States and Mexico boundary just after the war between those two countries. Although primarily a military man, Emory took a lively interest in the natural history of the border states, and

Janice Bowers

he encouraged and supported the various botanists under his command. Emory's contribution to their efforts is recognized and remembered in *Hyptis emoryi* and other plants.

SCIENTIFIC NAME	*Hyptis emoryi* Torr.
FAMILY	Mint
RANGE	Southern Arizona, southern California, and northwestern Mexico

93 · Broomrape

SCIENTIFIC NAME	*Orobanche cooperi* (Gray) Heller
FAMILY	Broomrape
RANGE	West Texas to Nevada, southeastern California, and northwestern Mexico

Broomrape, a parasite, depends entirely on its host plants for sugars, water, and nutrients. Parasitic plants attach themselves to their hosts by means of special conducting tubes called haustoria. (Like most other parasites, broomrape lacks true roots.) Hosts of broomrape in the desert are mostly various shrubs in the sunflower family, particularly the bur-sages (*Ambrosia* spp.) and the burrobushes (*Hymenoclea* spp.). Secretions from the roots of host plants stimulate broomrape seeds to germinate. This keeps them from germinating on the wrong host or in the absence of a host altogether.

Bruce Griffin

94 · Desert Aster

When is an aster not an aster? When it's a *Machaeranthera*. In the Southwest, asters are mainly perennial herbs of mountain meadows and forests, whereas the *Machaeranthera*s are mostly annuals of roadsides and other disturbed habitats in the desert and woodland. In comparison to the moisture-loving asters, the various species of *Machaeranthera* show marked adaptations to their arid habitat, including fewer and smaller leaves and shorter lifespans. The tooth-grinding name *Machaeranthera* means "sword-anther" and refers to the elongated tips of the anthers that can be seen under magnification. Desert aster blooms mostly in the fall, though occasionally in spring.

Rick and Nora Bowers

SCIENTIFIC NAME	*Machaeranthera canescens* (Pursh) Gray
FAMILY	Sunflower
RANGE	New Mexico to Nevada and southern Arizona

95 · Mojave Aster

Steven P. McLaughlin

The lavender flowers of Mojave aster measure up to two inches across, quite large for a desert wildflower. Usually a spring bloomer, Mojave aster sometimes flowers in the fall as well. Occasionally you may find black caterpillars with gray and orange stripes on the foliage—these will most likely be the larvae of the desert checkerspot (*Charidryas neumoegeni*), a pretty orange butterfly common after wet winters. Desert checkerspot caterpillars specialize on Mojave asters and one or two other spring-blooming wildflowers. Checkerspots and other desert butterflies visit Mojave aster for nectar during the brief desert spring. Mojave aster occurs on rocky slopes and flats.

SCIENTIFIC NAME	*Xylorhiza tortifolia* (Torr. & Gray) Greene
FAMILY	Sunflower
RANGE	Utah, Nevada, western Arizona, and southeastern California

96 · New Mexico Thistle

The extravagantly large flower heads of New Mexico thistle attract a variety of pollinators: bumblebees, carpenter bees, butterflies, and beetles luxuriate amid the lavender flowers. Seeds of New Mexico thistle do not go unappreciated, either, and goldfinches winnowing seeds from the fluff are a common sight in the desert. Thistle seeds are particularly well adapted for dispersing long distances from the parent plant. The many plumelike hairs help the seeds float in the wind, and the tall stems provide an excellent launching site. New Mexico thistle blooms in the spring and occurs on rocky slopes and along roadsides.

Rick and Nora Bowers

SCIENTIFIC NAME	*Cirsium neomexicanum* Gray
FAMILY	Sunflower
RANGE	Colorado to Nevada, southern California, Arizona, and New Mexico

97 · Parish Larkspur

SCIENTIFIC NAME	*Delphinium parishii* Gray
FAMILY	Crowfoot
RANGE	California and Arizona

Larkspur is tailor-made for bee pollination. The flowers are blue, a favorite color of bees, and only a strong insect—such as a bumblebee—can push apart the petals to get at the nectar. In foraging for nectar, bumblebees become dusted with pollen to carry to the next blossom. Larkspurs hide their nectar in the spur at the back of the flower to protect it from insects that are not legitimate pollinators. A small insect might otherwise crawl into the flower and drink the nectar without pollinating the stigmas. Parish larkspur blooms in the spring and grows on rocky slopes.

Steven P. McLaughlin

98 · Desert Lupine

Seeds of desert lupine germinate on as little as half an inch of fall or winter rain, so even during a spring when the wildflower display is poor, you might be able to find masses of this blue-flowered lupine on highway shoulders. As many as ten species of bees, including bumblebees and honeybees, visit and pollinate the flowers of desert lupine. When ripe, the pods explode and fling their seeds into the air. Desert lupine grows at somewhat higher elevations than Arizona lupine, often on rocky slopes. In good years the blue flowers mix colorfully with the gold ones of Mexican poppy and the magenta blossoms of owl's clover.

C. Allan Morgan

SCIENTIFIC NAME	*Lupinus sparsiflorus* Benth.
FAMILY	Pea
RANGE	Southern California to western New Mexico

99 · Blue Phacelia

The more than 100 species of phacelia in the western United States are difficult to distinguish; ripe seeds are usually necessary for precise identification. Pale blue flowers and weak, straggling stems, however, set this phacelia apart from other desert phacelias. It commonly grows tangled among the lower branches of shrubs along washes or at roadsides. Like wild heliotrope, another phacelia, blue phacelia is a spring-blooming annual.

C. Allan Morgan

SCIENTIFIC NAME	*Phacelia distans* Benth.
FAMILY	Waterleaf
RANGE	Nevada, Arizona, and California

100 · Chia

Chia is easily recognized by the tiny blue flowers aggregated in several balls along the stem. Like most members of the mint family, chia has square stems. In general, mints have a clean, fresh odor: they smell good, as do peppermint, oregano, and lavender. Chia, however, smells distinctly skunky. Southwestern Indians harvested large quantities of chia seed by beating the ripe seed heads over flat, tightly woven baskets. The powdered seeds were added to water to make a nutritious drink or gruel. When moistened by rainfall, the entire seed develops a gelatinous coating that is believed to facilitate germination. Chia blooms in the spring and grows in washes and along roadsides.

Rick & Nora Bowers

SCIENTIFIC NAME	*Salvia columbariae* Benth.
FAMILY	Mint
RANGE	Southern Nevada, Arizona, and California

SUGGESTED READING

No field guide can include every wildflower in an area as rich in plant species as the Southwest. You may want to supplement this book with other wildflower identification guides, including:

Bowers, J. E. *One Hundred Roadside Wildflowers of Southwest Woodlands.* Tucson: Western National Parks Association, 1987.

Dodge, N. N. *Flowers of the Southwest Deserts.* Tucson: Western National Parks Association, 1985.

Munz, P. A. *California Desert Wildflowers.* Berkeley: University of California Press, 1962.

Niehaus, T. F. *Peterson Field Guide to Southwestern and Texas Wildflowers.* Boston: Houghton Mifflin Co., 1998.

Phillips, A. M. III. *Grand Canyon Wildflowers.* Grand Canyon: Grand Canyon Natural History Association, 1995.

Quinn, M. *Wildflowers of the Desert Southwest.* Tucson: Rio Nuevo Publishers, 2000.

Spellenberg, R. *Sonoran Desert Wildflowers.* Guilford, Conn.: Globe Pequot Press, 2003.

Readers with some training in botany will find the following manuals indispensable for identifying Southwest wildflowers:

Benson, L. *The Cacti of Arizona.* Rev., 3rd ed. Tucson: University of Arizona Press, 1969.

Benson, L. *The Cacti of the United States and Canada.* Stanford: Stanford University Press, 1982.

Benson, L. and R. A. Darrow. *Trees and Shrubs of the Southwestern Deserts.* 3rd ed. Tucson: University of Arizona Press, 1981.

Epple, A. O. *A Field Guide to the Plants of Arizona.* Guilford, Conn.: Globe Pequot Press, 1995.

Kearney, T. H. and R. H. Peebles. *Arizona Flora.* 2nd ed., with supplement by J. T. Howell, E. McClintock and others. Berkeley: University of California Press, 1960.

Martin, W. C., and C. R. Hutchins. *A Flora of New Mexico.* 2 vols. Port Jervis, N.Y.: J. Cramer, 1980.

Shreve, F. and I. L. Wiggins. *Vegetation and Flora of the Sonoran Desert*. 2 vols. Stanford: Stanford University Press, 1964.

Turner, R. M., J. E. Bowers, T. L. Burgess. *Sonoran Desert Plants: An Ecological Atlas*. Tucson: University of Arizona Press, 2005.

Readers who want to learn more about Southwest habitats might find the following books of interest:

Alcock, J. *Sonoran Desert Spring*. Chicago: University of Chicago Press, 1985.

Bowers, J. E. *Seasons of Wind: A Naturalist's Look at the Plant Life of Southwestern Sand Dunes*. Flagstaff: Northland Press, 1986.

Gehlbach, F. R. *Mountain Islands and Desert Seas: A Natural History of U. S.–Mexican Borderlands*. College Station: Texas A&M University Press, 1981.

A more technical approach to Southwest habitats is taken by the authors of the following books, but the layperson should be able to find much of value in them:

Brown, D. E., ed. *"Biotic Communities of the American Southwest — United States and Mexico. Desert Plants"* 4:1–132. Superior: Boyce Thompson Southwestern Arboretum, 1982.

McGinnies, W. G. *Discovering the Desert*. Tucson: University of Arizona Press, 1981.

Turner, R. M., J. E. Bowers, J. R. Hastings, and R. H. Webb. *The Changing Mile Revisited*. Tucson: University of Arizona Press, 2003.

Neither the author nor the publisher endorse the use of any medicinal or edible wild plant discussed in this book. However, readers seeking further information on beneficial plants of the Southwest might enjoy:

Moore, M. *Medicinal Plants of the Mountain West*. Rev. Ed. Santa Fe: Museum of New Mexico Press, 2003.

Nabhan, G. P. *Gathering the Desert*. Tucson: University of Arizona Press, 1987.

INDEX